PRAY WITHOUT CEASING

Bible Stories for Kids about Prayer

JARED DEES

_____

For more information visit jareddees.com.

Paperback: ISBN 978-1-7332048-8-0
eBook: ISBN 978-1-7332048-9-7

First Edition

CONTENTS

Part Three
PRAYERS OF THANKSGIVING

Part Four
PRAYERS OF PRAISE

Part Five
PRAYERS OF BLESSING

INTRODUCTION

While we may not be able to see God, we can always speak with him. Speaking with God is, of course, called prayer. We can speak to God at any time, about anything, and he hears us. While we may not always hear answers in the form of spoken words, he is there, listening and seeking to extend his blessing upon us.

Saint Paul urges Christians in his first letter to the Thessalonians to "pray without ceasing." These are such wise words for us today. Pray every day with humility and hope in the Lord. God is not far off and distant. God is close to us, and he wants to get closer through prayer.

The many stories in this book will teach you how to pray. They provide examples of men and women in the Bible who looked to the Lord for help and gave thanks and praise for the blessings in their lives. Their stories unlock the keys to a strong spiritual life.

The stories are divided into two sections. The first set of stories will help you establish a consistent habit of prayer. Hopefully, after reading these stories, you will be able to pick the best time and place for you to spend in prayer. The second set of stories in this book provides examples of the five forms of prayer. Most people think of prayer only as us asking God for help, but you will find that you have much more to say to God in prayer.

We will focus on five ways to pray in this book:

1. Petition: Ask God to help you.

2. Intercession: Ask God to help others.

3. Thanksgiving: Give God gratitude.

4. Praise: Express God's goodness.

5. Blessing: Invoke God's grace.

After you establish a consistent prayer practice, spend time praying using each of these five forms of prayer. Read the stories in this book for examples of what to say and how to say it.

God is listening. He wants to hear your voice. Pray today, tomorrow, and the next day. Pray nonstop. Pray without ceasing, and put your confidence in the Lord.

> *"Rejoice always, pray without ceasing, give thanks in all circumstances; for this is the will of God in Christ Jesus for you."*
>
> *1 Thessalonians 5:16–18*

WHEN AND WHERE TO PRAY

Jesus told his disciples, "Whenever you pray, go into your room and shut the door and pray to your Father who is in secret; and your Father who sees in secret will reward you" (Matthew 6:6).

The stories you will read in this section show people encountering the Lord in quiet, private places, just as Jesus told his disciples to do. Following the example of each of these individuals, find a good place and a good time each day to spend with the Lord in prayer.

SAMUEL HEARS GOD'S CALL

1 Samuel 3

Our God is not far away or silent. He speaks to us, but how can we hear him? This is the story of the first time the prophet Samuel heard the voice of the Lord. He was young, but that didn't stop him from seeking to serve God.

As you read this story, pay attention to where Samuel was when he heard God's voice.

There once was a righteous boy named Samuel. When he was still very young, his mother gave him to the care of a high priest named Eli so that he could serve the Lord. Eli was old and nearly blind. He needed Samuel's help for many things.

At the end of a long day of work, Samuel was sleeping in the temple when he heard a voice calling to him, "Samuel! Samuel!"

"Here I am," he said. He got up and ran to his master, Eli. "Here I am, for you called me."

But Eli was confused. "I did not call for you. Lie down again."

So Samuel went back to sleep. Then he heard the voice again say, "Samuel!"

He got up quickly and ran back to his master. "Here I am, for you called me."

Eli said, "I did not call you. Go lie down again and get some sleep."

Then he heard the voice a third time and came running to his master once more.

This time, Eli realized what was happening. "Go, lie down; and if he calls you, you shall say, 'Speak, Lord, for your servant is listening.'"

Samuel was in disbelief. Seeing or hearing God's voice was very uncommon. Yet he wanted to serve his master well. He went back to lie down.

"Samuel! Samuel!" said the voice of the Lord.

"Speak, for your servant is listening," the boy said in reply.

Then the Lord spoke to young Samuel for the first time. It was the first of many times that the Lord God spoke to Samuel. Each time, Samuel listened and sought to follow the Lord's instructions.

REFLECTION QUESTIONS

Samuel was able to recognize the voice as the Lord speaking to him because of the help of his master, Eli. Who has helped you listen for the voice of the Lord in your life?

Samuel heard the voice of God while alone in a quiet place. Where can you go to find a quiet place for prayer?

While it may be uncommon for us to hear the actual voice of the Lord, what are some of the ways people listen to God in prayer?

ELIJAH ENCOUNTERS GOD IN THE SILENCE

1 Kings 19:9–12

It can be difficult to find quiet time. It is a challenge for everyone, both adults and kids. But finding that quiet time for prayer is very important. In this story, the prophet Elijah travels to a mountain, where he will encounter God's presence.

As you read this story, pay attention to the way Elijah finally experiences God's presence.

Elijah took shelter in a cave on a mountain named Horeb (also called Mount Sinai).

While resting in the cave, he heard the word of the Lord saying, "Go out of the cave and stand on the mountain, because I am about to pass by."

A great wind blew through the cave. The wind was so strong that rocks broke off of the mountain.

But the Lord was not in the wind.

Then Elijah felt an earthquake shake the ground.

But the Lord was not in the earthquake.

Then a fire erupted on the mountain. It burned hot and bright.

But the Lord was not in the fire.

Then there was silence.

When Elijah heard the silence, he wrapped his face in his cloak. He went out and stood at the entrance to the cave.

For the Lord was waiting for him in the silence.

REFLECTION QUESTIONS

How did Elijah finally experience God's presence?

What are some of the distractions that make it hard for you to pray to God?

Where and when can you find silence during the day?

DANIEL PRAYS EVERY DAY

Daniel 6

After the Jews were conquered by the Babylonians, they were forced to live away from their home. It was not easy to continue to worship God, and some of them had to do so in secret.

As you read this story, pay attention to the reason Daniel is punished by the king.

King Darius appointed three men to preside over Babylon. Among these men was a Jew named Daniel. Daniel was very successful, but the other two men became jealous. They sought to kill him.

They followed Daniel and saw him praying to God regularly, three times a day, every day. So the other two men persuaded the king to write a law in the kingdom that no one should worship any God but the king of Babylon.

King Darius was very pleased with Daniel's work, so when Daniel was accused of praying to the God of

Israel, he was greatly saddened. He did not want to punish Daniel, but there was no way for him to change the law now that it was written.

In sadness, he had Daniel thrown into a lions' den to be killed and eaten. "May your God, whom you faithfully serve, save you!" he said as they rolled a stone over the entrance to the den.

The king went and fasted that evening and barely slept at all. As soon as the sun rose, he got up and hurried to the lions' den. He cried out, "O Daniel, has your God saved you from the lions?"

Then he heard Daniel's voice, "O king, live forever! My God has sent his angel to shut the lions' mouths. They did not hurt me, because I was found blameless before God and before you. I have done no wrong."

The king was filled with joy. He made a new decree that all in the land should tremble and fear before the God of Daniel, "for he is the living God, enduring forever. His kingdom shall never be destroyed."

REFLECTION QUESTIONS

Why was Daniel sentenced to death?

Daniel prayed three times a day, every day. How can you find a regular time to pray each day?

When do you have opportunities to pray in public, even if it makes other people uncomfortable?

JESUS PRAYS IN A QUIET PLACE

Mark 1:32–39

Jesus taught us how to pray. He said, "But whenever you pray, go into your room and shut the door and pray to your Father who is in secret; and your Father who sees in secret will reward you" (Matthew 6:6). He also showed us how to pray. As you can imagine, Jesus was very busy. A lot of people wanted his attention.

As you read this story, pay attention to how Jesus made time for prayer.

Jesus was very busy. He often taught and spoke in the synagogue, where people came to worship God.

One evening, he left the synagogue to stay at the home of his friend and follower Peter. Peter's mother-in-law was there. She was sick with a fever.

Jesus walked up to her bed and took her hand. He helped her up. The fever immediately left her, and she was better again. She felt so good that she made them all dinner.

Other people brought their sick friends and family to Peter's house that night. Everyone in the entire town was waiting outside the door. Jesus healed many, many people that night.

Jesus woke up very early the next day, before the sunrise. He left the house to go find a place where he could be alone. There, he prayed.

Peter and Jesus's disciples arrived and interrupted Jesus's prayer.

"Everyone is looking for you," Peter said.

Jesus looked up at them and nodded his head. "Let us go on to the nearby villages, that I may preach there also. For this purpose I have come."

Jesus and his disciples left Peter's home and traveled to many other towns nearby so that Jesus could preach and teach in their synagogues.

REFLECTION QUESTIONS

Where and when did Jesus find time to pray?

What are some of the things that keep you the most busy?

Where and when can you find time to pray?

JESUS PRAYS FOR GOD'S WILL TO BE DONE

Matthew 26:36–45; Mark 14:32–41; Luke 22:39–46

The night before he died, Jesus went out to pray. He knew how difficult it was going to be to suffer and die on the cross.

He brought his disciples with him to pray in the garden, but their ability to pray was disappointing. As you read the story, pay attention to what Jesus says to the disciples when he finds them sleeping.

After sharing the Last Supper with his disciples, Jesus led them out to a garden called Gethsemane.

"Sit here while I go over there to pray," he told them. Then he asked Peter, James, and John to join him.

As they were walking, Jesus began to feel great sorrow and distress. "My soul is sorrowful, even to the point of death," he said. "Remain here and keep watch with me."

Then Jesus went on a little farther to be alone. He fell down to the ground and prayed, "My Father, if it is possible, let this cup pass from me."

He knew he would have to die for the sins of God's people. It was going to be very, very difficult. He continued to pray, "Yet not as I will, but as you will."

He got up and returned to find Peter, James, and John asleep. He woke Peter up and said, "So you could not keep watch with me for one hour? Watch and pray that you do not have to undergo such a challenge."

Peter was embarrassed but still very tired.

"The spirit is willing, but the body is weak," Jesus told him.

Jesus went off again to be alone and again prayed that the cup would pass from him. But again he said to God, "Your will be done!"

When he returned a second time, his disciples were sleeping again. Disappointed, Jesus went off to pray for a third time, saying the same prayer.

Then, for the third time, his disciples fell asleep.

He returned and woke them up. "Are you still sleeping? Behold, the hour is at hand when I will be handed over to sinners."

REFLECTION QUESTIONS

How do you think the disciples felt after Jesus woke them up for the third time?

What distracts you from staying focused during prayer?

What challenge would you like to avoid in your life? Would you be willing to tell God you will go through that challenge if it is his will?

THE FIVE WAYS TO PRAY

Prayer is the way we talk to God, but when we talk, what do we say? There are five different ways to pray:

1. Petition: Ask God to help you.

2. Intercession: Ask God to help others.

3. Thanksgiving: Give God gratitude.

4. Praise: Express God's goodness.

5. Blessing: Invoke God's grace.

The stories you will read in this collection provide examples of each of these forms of prayer and will guide you as you try each way to pray.

PRAYERS OF PETITION

The most common way for us to pray is to look to God for help. When we ask God for something, we are offering up a prayer of petition. God wants us to ask for his help. The only thing he asks for in return is the faith that he will answer us. The following stories offer examples of people who overcome doubt and remain faithful in their prayers to God.

One of the most significant prayers of petition we can offer is the request for forgiveness from God. No one is perfect. Only God is perfect, yet he is very merciful. The last few stories in this section show us how to humbly ask for God's forgiveness.

THE WIDOW'S PERSISTENT REQUEST

Luke 18:1-8

In this parable about prayer, Jesus encourages his disciples to be persistent. Too many times, we stop asking God for help because we give up or get distracted by other things in life.

As you read this parable, pay attention to what the widow did when the judge didn't give an answer to her request.

Jesus told his disciples a parable about their need to pray persistently and never lose heart.

There once was a judge who did not fear God. He was mean to people and very disrespectful.

There was a widow who often came to the judge to ask for help. A widow is a woman whose husband has died. She was the victim of a crime, but the criminal was not punished.

"Grant me justice against my opponent," she said to the judge.

He refused her request.

She asked him again, but he still refused to help her.

The more she asked, however, the more he started to change his mind.

He thought to himself, "Though I have no fear of God and no respect for this widow, she won't stop bothering me. I will grant her justice so that she will stop coming to me for help."

Jesus explained this parable to his disciples, saying, "Listen to what the unjust judge says. And will not God grant justice to the chosen ones who cry to him day and night? Will he delay long in helping them? I tell you, he will quickly grant justice to those who keep asking him for help."

REFLECTION QUESTIONS

Why did the judge grant the widow justice?

Have you ever asked God for help without giving up, like the widow in the parable?

What prayer request can you ask of God repeatedly, starting today?

THE PERSISTENT PLEA OF A FRIEND

Luke 11:5–13

Jesus's disciples asked him to teach them to pray. He told them to pray the prayer we know as the Lord's Prayer or the Our Father, then he told them a short parable about persistence in prayer.

As you read this story, pay attention to the reason the neighbor finally helps his friend.

Jesus told a parable to his disciples.

He told them that a person heard a knock at the door in the middle of the night.

He got up and went to the door and saw a neighbor standing there.

"What do you need?" he asked the person at the door.

"Friend, please give me three loaves of bread. Another friend has arrived at my house, and I have nothing to give him," he replied.

"Go away. It is the middle of the night, and I've already locked the door. My children are in bed sleeping. I cannot prepare anything for you right now," he said. Then he shut the door and went back to sleep.

The neighbor continued to knock and ask for help. The man was tired and just wanted to sleep, so he eventually got up and brought the neighbor some food to share.

Then Jesus explained this parable further, saying, "Ask, and it will be given you; search, and you will find; knock, and the door will be opened for you. For everyone who asks receives, and everyone who searches finds, and for everyone who knocks, the door will be opened."

Then he gave one more metaphor. "If your children asked you for a fish, would you give them a snake? If they asked you for an egg, would you give them a scorpion? Of course not! In the same way, your heavenly Father will give you the Holy Spirit if you ask him!"

REFLECTION QUESTIONS

Why did the person in the story finally help their neighbor out?

What can you pray for persistently until God answers your prayer?

What are you asking God for right now, and what do you think he will give to you in return?

KING SOLOMON PRAYS FOR WISDOM

1 Kings 3:3–15; 2 Chronicles 1:1–13

King Solomon was the son of David and a great king over Israel. He was known especially for his great wisdom, which was a gift from God.

As you read this story, pay attention to what God promises to King Solomon after he prays for wisdom.

King Solomon went to Gibeon to offer a sacrifice to the Lord. God appeared to him in a dream there and said, "Ask what I should give to you. I will grant you whatever you ask."

Solomon answered in prayer, "You have shown great and steadfast love to your servant my father David. He was faithful to you and righteous. And now, Lord, you have made me, your servant, king in place of my father. I am still so young. There is so much for me to learn. There are so many people that I am to rule over as your servant."

Solomon paused for a moment, thinking about what he should ask for from the Lord. Then he prayed, "Give your servant wisdom to govern your people and discern between good and evil."

God was pleased with this prayer. "Because you have asked for wisdom," he said, "and not for a long life, great wealth, or the death of your enemies, I will answer your prayer. I give you a wise and discerning mind like no one before you or after you. I will also give the things you have not asked for. I will give you wealth and honor all of your life. And if you walk in my ways and keep my commandments, I will also give you long life."

Solomon woke up and returned to Jerusalem to pray in thanksgiving to God for these many gifts.

REFLECTION QUESTIONS

Why did Solomon ask for wisdom from God?

If God told you he would give you anything you asked for, what would you ask of him?

What are some of the gifts that God has already given to you? How can you show him gratitude for these gifts?

THE LEPER ASKS FOR HEALING

Matthew 8:1–4; Mark 1:40–45; Luke 5:12–15

There were many diseases in the ancient world without cures yet. Leprosy was a disease that caused someone's skin to break out in large bumps. It was very contagious, so anyone with leprosy was sent away from the communities to live in isolation.

As you read this story, pay attention to how the leper asks Jesus to heal him.

Jesus came down from a mountain after teaching the crowds of people that followed him. Then a man with leprosy walked up to him. Jesus's disciples and those around him were anxious. They were afraid of getting sick, too.

The leper said, "Lord, if you choose, you can make me clean."

Jesus felt pity for the leper. He reached out his hand to touch him and said, "I do choose. Be made clean!"

Immediately, the man's skin changed, and he was healed. The leprosy was gone!

Jesus told the man to go and show himself to a priest for inspection so that he would be allowed back into the community.

He also warned him not to say anything to anyone, but the man couldn't keep the story of this miracle to himself. He told everyone about the miracle. People started to come from all over to seek out Jesus to be healed as well.

REFLECTION QUESTIONS

How did the leper show humility and faith when he asked Jesus to heal him?

Who do you know that could pray for Jesus's healing touch?

Why is it hard to say to God in prayer, "If you choose, you can . . ." instead of just asking him to help or heal you?

THE BLIND MAN ASKS JESUS TO HELP HIM SEE

Mark 10:46–52

Jesus healed many people who were blind in the Bible. The blind were often begging for money, because their lack of sight made it impossible for them to find work to earn money.

As you read this story, pay attention to the way Bartimaeus shows he has strong faith in Jesus.

Jesus and his disciples left the city of Jericho, with a large crowd of people following behind them. As they left the city, a blind beggar named Bartimaeus was sitting on the side of the road.

"Jesus of Nazareth is coming this way," the beggar heard someone say nearby.

When Bartimaeus heard this, he shouted out, "Jesus, Son of David, have mercy on me!"

"Be quiet!" said the people nearby.

"Shh!" ordered some others.

But the blind man shouted even louder, "Son of David, have mercy on me!"

Jesus stood still. "Call him here," he said.

The people called the blind man over, saying, "Take heart; get up, he is calling you."

Bartimaeus sprang up and left his cloak behind as he made his way toward Jesus.

"What do you want me to do for you?" Jesus asked Bartimaeus.

"My teacher, let me see again," he replied.

"Go," Jesus said. "Your faith has made you well."

Suddenly, Bartimaeus could see again. He jumped with joy, and tears came streaming down his face.

Jesus continued along the road with the crowd and his disciples. Bartimaeus followed him along the way toward Jerusalem.

REFLECTION QUESTIONS

How did Bartimaeus show courage and faith in asking Jesus for healing?

Imagine if Jesus asked you the same question he asked Bartimaeus: "What do you want me to do for you?" What would you pray in response?

Who encourages you to pray and prays with and for you the most?

ZECHARIAH PRAYS WITH SOME DOUBT

Luke 1:5–25, 57–80

○‿○

Sometimes we pray in desperation but then have doubts that God will actually answer our prayers. That was the experience of Zechariah, who did not believe that his prayers could be answered.

As you read this story, pay attention to the way Zechariah reacts when the angel tells him his prayer will be answered.

Zechariah was a priest. His wife's name was Elizabeth. They were good and holy people. They followed the commandments and set a great example for the people that knew them. Sadly, however, they were unable to have any children. They prayed for a child as a gift from God.

Zechariah was working as a priest in the Temple one day while people were praying outside. He offered incense to the Lord, and suddenly, an angel appeared to him.

"Do not be afraid, Zechariah, for your prayers have been heard. Your wife Elizabeth will have a son, and you will name him John," said the angel.

Zechariah was in shock, both at the sight of the angel and at the angel's words.

"You will be filled with joy, and many others will rejoice in the birth of your son. He will be filled with the Holy Spirit and turn many people back to the Lord their God. He will prepare the way for the Lord," the angel continued.

But Zechariah was in disbelief. "How can I know this is true? I am an old man, and my wife is old, too."

"I am Gabriel. I stand in the presence of God, who sent me to you to bring this good news. But since you did not believe in my words, you will become unable to speak until the birth of your son," said the angel Gabriel.

Outside, the people started to worry about Zechariah. He had been in the Temple a long time. When he finally came out, they saw that he could not speak. They realized he must have had some kind of vision.

He returned home, and soon his wife became pregnant. "Look what the Lord has done for me," she said excitedly to Zechariah. "He has looked upon me with his favor and blessed me."

Many months later, Elizabeth gave birth to a son. Her neighbors and relatives rejoiced with her, knowing that

God had blessed her in her old age. They suggested that the boy be named Zechariah after his father.

"No," she said. "We will name him John."

"But no one in your family is named John. Why would you name him that?" they said.

Zechariah was still unable to speak after he doubted the angel's words. When the people came to him to ask about the name of the child, he wrote on a tablet, "His name is John."

He did this according to the angel's instructions. Suddenly, he was able to speak again. He immediately praised God not only for his answered prayer but for God's great plan for his son, John the Baptist.

REFLECTION QUESTIONS

What did Zechariah say when the angel of God told him his prayer would be answered?

What have you been praying for lately? Would you have doubts if you found that God had answered your prayer? Why or why not?

Elizabeth and Zechariah's family and friends rejoiced when they saw that God had answered their prayers. Who would rejoice with you if God were to answer one of your prayers?

THE TAX COLLECTOR'S HUMBLE PRAYER

Luke 18:9–14

When we pray, we must be humble before God. He does not respond to our prayers because of how holy or special we are. He responds to us when we pray in humility and faith that we need him in our lives. Jesus warned us to be careful not to let pride influence the way we pray.

As you read this story, pay attention to the difference between the way these two men speak to God in prayer.

Jesus told his disciples a parable about two men who went up to the Temple to pray.

One of the men was a Pharisee. Pharisees were experts in God's Law. They were supposed to be holy and respectable people.

The other man was a tax collector. The Jews had to give money to tax collectors to give to their Roman rulers. People did not like tax collectors, because they often took more than they were supposed to collect. They kept this extra money for themselves.

The Pharisee stood alone in the Temple and prayed, "God, I thank you that I am not like other people who break the law, or even like that tax collector over there."

The Pharisee looked back at the tax collector and shook his head, then continued his prayer, "I fast by not eating any food twice a week. I give ten percent of all the money I make to the Temple."

The tax collector was standing far from the Pharisee. His head was bowed. He would not even look up to heaven while he prayed. Instead, he beat his chest with his fist, praying, "God, be merciful to me, a sinner!"

Jesus explained this parable to his disciples. He said to them, "The tax collector went home closer to God than the Pharisee. For all who pridefully exalt themselves will be humbled, but all who humble themselves will be exalted."

REFLECTION QUESTIONS

What was wrong with the way the Pharisee prayed, and how was the tax collector's prayer different?

Do you ever mistakenly think you deserve God's help because of how good or holy you are? How can you be more humble in prayer instead?

When was the last time you asked God to be merciful on you as a sinner?

DAVID PRAYS FOR FORGIVENESS

2 Samuel 12; Psalm 51

King David was a great man, but he committed a horrible sin. He wanted to marry a woman named Bathsheba, but she was already married to another man. David had her husband killed in battle so that he could marry her.

In this story, David seeks forgiveness from God for his sin. As you read this story, pay attention to the way he asks for God's forgiveness.

When God's prophet Nathan heard of what David had done to Bathsheba's husband, he approached David and spoke on God's behalf.

"God made you king," he said. "God saved you from your enemies. God gave you many things, yet you still want more. Why have you done evil in the sight of the Lord?"

"I have sinned against the Lord!" said David. He was very sad for his grave mistake.

Then King David prayed, "Have mercy on me, God, according to your steadfast love and abundant mercy. Cleanse me from my sin. For I know my mistake, and it is ever before me. Create in me a clean heart, O God, and put a new and right spirit within me."

The prophet Nathan responded, "Now the Lord has put away your sin. You shall not die, but you will suffer the loss of a child because of this sin."

David did lose his first son with Bathsheba, but their second son, Solomon, became the next king of God's people.

REFLECTION QUESTIONS

How did King David ask for God's forgiveness?

What does it feel like when you do something wrong?

What should we say to God when we seek his forgiveness?

THE PRODIGAL SON'S PRAYER FOR FORGIVENESS

Luke 15:11–32

Jesus told a story that we know as the Parable of the Prodigal Son. It is about a young son who wastes his share of his father's property. The father in the parable is God our Father. The son in the story is a person that sins but then seeks God's forgiveness.

As you read this story, pay attention to the words the son says in his apology to the father.

A man had two sons. Normally, a father would pass on his money and property to his sons after his death, but the younger son asked his father to give him his share early.

The younger son took all this money and traveled far away. He wasted it all away until he had nothing left. He was poor and hungry.

He went to a farmer and asked him for a job. The farmer sent him to take care of the pigs. Even the pigs ate better food than the young man was able to eat.

The son realized his mistake. He thought he could go home and ask his father to hire him as a servant. He planned to say these words:

"Father, I have sinned against heaven and against you. I no longer deserve to be called your son. Treat me as you would treat one of your hired workers."

When he returned home, his father saw him coming from a distance. The father ran to greet his son. He wrapped his arms around him. Then the young man said, "Father, I have sinned against heaven and against you. I no longer deserve to be called your son."

Instead of being angry, the father was filled with joy. He threw a big party to welcome his son home, because his son was lost, but now he was back again.

REFLECTION QUESTIONS

How did the son seek the father's forgiveness in the parable?

What similar prayer could we pray to God to seek forgiveness for our sins?

Is there anyone who you need to forgive, as the father forgives the son in this story?

PRAYERS OF INTERCESSION

A prayer of intercession is very similar to a prayer of petition, except for one thing: instead of asking God for something for ourselves, a prayer of intercession asks God for something for someone else. We have the opportunity to pray for family, friends, and even people we do not know or do not even like.

As you read these stories, think about the ways you can pray for others who are in need of help or healing from God.

MOSES ASKS FOR FORGIVENESS FOR GOD'S PEOPLE

Exodus 32

God called Moses to lead the people of Israel out of Egypt, and then he gave Moses many laws for his people to follow. The first of these commandments was to worship only God and no idols. The Israelites, however, were used to worshipping images instead of a God they could not see.

As you read this story, pay attention to the way Moses intercedes for the people of Israel after they have sinned.

Moses spent a long time on Mount Sinai, receiving instructions from God. God gave him the Ten Commandments and wrote them on stone tablets for Moses to bring down to the people of Israel.

At the bottom of the mountain, however, the people had become impatient. Moses had been gone for a long time. They went to Moses's brother, Aaron, and asked him to create for them an image of a god for them to worship.

Aaron told them to give him all their gold earrings and necklaces. He melted them down and shaped them into a statue of a calf. He saw that the people liked the statue, so he built an altar for them to worship it.

God became enraged. He said to Moses, "Go down this mountain at once! Your people have already disobeyed me and built an image to worship other gods. They say that the golden calf led them out of Egypt! I will bring disaster upon them for this!"

But Moses prayed for the people and spoke in defense of them. "O Lord, why does your wrath burn hot against your people whom you brought out of the land of Egypt? Turn away from your anger. Change your mind, and do not bring disaster upon them. Remember Abraham, Isaac, and Jacob and how you promised to give them many descendants."

The Lord heard Moses, and he did change his mind. He did not bring the total disaster that he had planned upon the people.

Moses went down from the mountain with the two tablets containing the Ten Commandments. As soon as he saw the Israelites singing and dancing around the golden calf, he threw the tablets and broke them. He melted down the golden calf and destroyed it. He was very angry with them but relieved that God did not completely destroy them.

"You have sinned a great sin," he said to the people. "But I will continue to pray that God will forgive you."

REFLECTION QUESTIONS

What did Moses say to God in defense of the people of Israel?

Who do you know that has made a mistake who you can pray for?

Who prays for you when you make mistakes?

KING HEZEKIAH PRAYS FOR ISRAEL'S PROTECTION

2 Kings 18–19

The Assyrians came with armies to conquer God's people. First they conquered the northern Kingdom of Israel, then they moved on to overthrow King Hezekiah of Judah in Jerusalem.

As you read this story, pay attention to the way King Hezekiah asks for God's protection of the city of Jerusalem.

The Assyrian army arrived outside the gates of Jerusalem. Their emissary announced to the people of Judah, "Thus says the great king of Assyria: on whom do you rely that you have rebelled against me? Your God? Your king? Ha! Do not let Hezekiah deceive you. Your Lord will not protect you."

The people were silent, for King Hezekiah had told them not to respond.

The king was faithful to God. He went to the Temple and prayed, "O Lord the God of Israel, who is enthroned above the great angels, you are God, you alone over all the kingdoms of the earth. You have made heaven and earth. Listen to the words of the Assyrians, who mock you. They have conquered so many lands, and now they approach us. O Lord our God, save us, I pray you, from the hand of the Assyrians, so that all the kingdoms of the earth may know that you, O Lord, are God alone."

The prophet Isaiah heard Hezekiah's prayer. He came to the king and proclaimed, "Thus says the Lord, the God of Israel: I have heard your prayer to me about the Assyrians. They have mocked the Lord! I know when they sit and when they stand. I know when they come and when they go. I have heard their arrogance. I will turn them back the way they came!"

That night an angel of the Lord attacked the Assyrian armies. Those that survived fled back to their land. The Kingdom of Judah had been protected by God.

REFLECTION QUESTIONS

In what way did King Hezekiah ask for God's help? How can we pray in a similar way?

What can you bring to the Lord in prayer today to ask for his help and protection?

Who helps you understand God's will for you as the prophet Isaiah did in this story?

THE CANAANITE MOTHER ASKS JESUS TO HEAL HER DAUGHTER

Matthew 15:21–28; Mark 7:24–30

Jesus was one of the people of Israel. They were called the Jews, and they were God's people. The Gentiles were people who were not Jewish. The Jews expected the Messiah to help and save them and restore the kingdom. They did not think this applied to the Gentiles. God had a different plan.

As you read this story, pay attention to the reason Jesus finally answers the Canaanite woman and heals her daughter.

Jesus and his disciples traveled to a place where mostly Gentiles lived. A Canaanite woman from the area saw them and shouted to Jesus, "Have mercy on me, Lord, Son of David! My daughter is tormented by a demon."

At first Jesus did not answer her, but she kept shouting after him.

Jesus's disciples said to him, "Send her away. She keeps shouting at us."

Jesus answered the woman, "I was sent only to the lost sheep of the house of Israel."

Still she persisted. She ran up to Jesus and knelt down before him. "Lord, help me," she said.

"Is it fair to take the food of children and throw it to the dogs?" he said. By this he meant that he was sent first to the people of Israel, while she was one of the Gentiles and was not Jewish.

"Yes, Lord, but even the dogs eat the crumbs that fall from their masters' table," she replied humbly.

Jesus answered, "Woman, great is your faith! Let it be done for you as you wish."

Her daughter was healed at that moment.

REFLECTION QUESTIONS

Why did Jesus heal the woman's daughter?

Who do you know and love that needs this same persistence and confidence that Jesus can help or heal them?

What gives you confidence that Jesus can help those you pray for?

THE CENTURION ASKS JESUS TO HEAL HIS SERVANT

Matthew 8:5–13

The Romans ruled over the land of Israel at the time of Jesus, and there were many Roman soldiers stationed in Judea. These Romans worshipped Roman gods, yet the centurion in this story had faith in Jesus Christ.

As you read this story, pay attention to the faith and humility that the centurion shows in Jesus, even though he is not Jewish or one of Jesus's followers.

As Jesus entered Capernaum, there was a Roman centurion who approached him, pleading for help. A centurion was a commander of one hundred soldiers in the Roman army.

"Lord, my servant is lying at home, paralyzed and in terrible distress," he said.

Jesus replied, "I will come and cure him."

The centurion was surprised by the response. "Lord, I am not worthy to have you come under my roof; but only speak the word, and my servant will be healed."

Jesus was amazed by the centurion's words. "Truly I tell you, in no one in Israel have I found such faith. Many will come from outside of Israel to eat with Abraham and Isaac and Jacob in the kingdom of heaven, while those who reject me will be thrown into darkness."

Jesus turned to the centurion and said, "Go; let it be done for you according to your faith."

The centurion's servant was healed in that hour.

REFLECTION QUESTIONS

How did the Roman centurion show his faith in Jesus?

How can we strengthen our faith in Jesus and have humility when we pray for someone?

In what ways do you or people you know need the healing power of Jesus?

JESUS PRAYS FOR THOSE WHO KILLED HIM

Matthew 27; Mark 15; Luke 23

Jesus instructed his disciples to "love your enemies and pray for those who persecute you" (Matthew 5:44) and "bless those who curse you, pray for those who abuse you" (Luke 6:28). He showed them how this was possible during his own persecution and death on the cross.

As you read this story, pay attention to the way Jesus reacts to the may people who hate and insult him.

Although there were many people who loved and supported Jesus, there were also people who hated him. The religious leaders of the Jews wanted to get rid of him because of the things he was teaching, so they brought him before the Roman governor, Pontius Pilate, with accusations that he claimed to be a king. Although the governor found him guilty of no crime, the crowds shouted, "Crucify him!" Pilate decided to sentence Jesus to death for fear of the crowds.

The soldiers led him away. They gathered around him and stripped him of his clothes. They put a purple robe around him and wove a crown of thorns for his head. They put a reed in his hand and began to shout insults at him.

"Hail, King of the Jews!" they shouted with laughter. Then they spit on him and struck him on the head. They put his own clothes back on him and placed a cross on his shoulders. They forced Jesus to carry the cross to the place where he would be crucified.

The soldiers nailed Jesus to the cross and raised him up. Above his head they placed a sign that read, "Jesus of Nazareth, King of the Jews," to mock him.

All the while, Jesus never spoke up or tried to stop them. Instead, he prayed for them from the cross, saying, "Father, forgive them; for they do not know what they are doing."

The insults continued. "He saved others, let him save himself," said the religious leaders there to witness his death.

The Roman soldiers joined in the mockery. "If you are the king of the Jews, save yourself!" they shouted.

Darkness came over the whole land, until 3 o'clock in the afternoon. Jesus cried out in a loud voice, "Father, into your hands I commend my spirit." Then he took his last breath.

One of the Roman soldiers, a centurion, stood by the cross, watching all that had taken place. He was so moved by what he saw that he proclaimed, "Certainly this man was innocent. He was the Son of God."

REFLECTION QUESTIONS

How did Jesus show love for his enemies and pray for those who abused him?

Why do you think Jesus didn't fight back against the people who killed him?

Is there anyone you do not like or that does not like you that you can pray for, as Jesus instructed?

THE CHURCH PRAYS FOR PETER IN PRISON

Acts 12:1–19

The Christian Church was growing in Jerusalem and the surrounding cities. King Herod and some other Jewish leaders sought to arrest and kill the Christian leaders.

As you read this story, pay attention to the people's reaction when their prayer for Peter's freedom is answered.

King Herod was an evil man. He arrested the apostle James and had him killed. The Christians in Jerusalem were very afraid.

Herod arrested Peter and put him in a heavily guarded prison. He locked him up with chains on both arms. Two soldiers were stationed next to him, but they were sleeping. Outside the cell, guards sat in watch over the front door.

Meanwhile, the Christian church members prayed fervently to God for Peter, their leader. They gathered together in secret to pray at the house of Mary, the mother of a disciple named John (also called Mark).

God answered the prayers of the church members. A bright light appeared in Peter's prison cell. An angel appeared to him and tapped him on the shoulder.

"Get up quickly," said the angel. Then the chains around Peter's wrists fell to the ground.

"Put on your sandals and wrap a cloak around you and follow me," the angel said.

At first, Peter thought he was having a dream. He followed the angel out of his cell and past all the guards. Then Peter realized that this was no vision. He was really being freed by the angel.

The angel led him to the iron gate leading out of the city. The gate opened on its own, and they went through without anyone noticing them. Then the angel left him.

"The Lord has sent an angel to rescue me," Peter said to himself. Then he ran to the house where the church members were gathered. He knocked on the door.

Inside, the Christians were still praying for Peter. He continued to knock, and finally a woman named Rhoda came to the door. Rhoda saw Peter, and her eyes filled with tears of joy. She was so excited she ran immediately back to tell the others, leaving Peter waiting at the door.

When the people heard this, they thought it was impossible, but Peter kept knocking.

Finally they opened the door. Everyone there was amazed. Their prayers had been answered. Peter was free!

REFLECTION QUESTIONS

Why do you think the Christians were so surprised to see Peter at their door?

Have you ever been surprised when God answered your prayers?

What impossible thing can you pray for today?

PRAYERS OF THANKSGIVING

At a very young age, you were taught to say thank you to someone who gives you a gift. God is a giver of so many great gifts. How do we say thank you to God? We offer up prayers of thanksgiving to him.

The following stories show people who were so grateful for God's gifts that they offered him their gratitude in prayer. This expression of gratitude is very pleasing to God. Your thanksgiving pleases God, too, so look for opportunities to say thank you in prayer whenever you can.

HANNAH PRAYS IN THANKSGIVING FOR HER SON

1 Samuel 1

Hannah was unable to have children. With no one else to turn to, she prayed to God for help. He answered her.

As you read this story, pay attention to the grateful sacrifice that Hannah makes to God for answering her prayer.

Hannah was desperate for a son, but she was unable to have children for many years. She was deeply saddened, and there was nothing her husband could do to comfort her. She would barely eat or drink because she was so sad.

Hannah went up to the temple of the Lord to pray. She knelt down and cried tears of sorrow. She was so sad that she could only whisper these words: "O Lord of hosts, if only you will look on the misery of your servant, and remember me, and not forget your servant, but give to me your servant a son, then I will dedicate him to you for all his life."

A priest named Eli watched her pray and came to make sure she was all right.

Hannah explained, "I am a woman deeply troubled. I have been pouring out my soul before the Lord."

Eli answered, "Go in peace; the God of Israel will grant the petition you have made of him."

"Let your servant find favor in your sight," she replied.

Hannah returned to her husband feeling much better. She was refreshed, with confidence in God. The Lord remembered her prayer, and she bore a son and named him Samuel.

Hannah kept her promise, and when Samuel was old enough, she took him to the temple for Eli to care for and train to become a priest.

She said to Eli, "I am the one that you saw whispering to the Lord in the temple. For this child I prayed; and the Lord has granted me the petition that I made to him. Therefore, as long as he lives, he is given to the Lord."

Hannah did not forget to give thanks to God for the gift of her son. As she left her son with Eli, she offered God a prayer of praise and thanksgiving.

"My heart exults in the Lord, my strength is exalted in my God," began her prayer. "The Lord will judge the ends of the earth; he will give strength to his king, and exalt the power of his anointed."

God bestowed many blessings on Samuel, and he became one of his greatest prophets. Samuel would anoint Israel's first king, Saul, and then later King David.

REFLECTION QUESTIONS

How did Hannah finally find comfort instead of sorrow?

What sacrifice or promise can you make to God for answering your prayer?

What prayers can you give thanks and praise to God for answering?

JONAH PRAYS FROM INSIDE THE WHALE

Jonah 1–2

Jonah was a prophet. God sent him to preach a message of repentance to the people of Nineveh. Jonah tried to avoid this calling from God, but God would not let him.

As you read this story, pay attention to the way that Jonah prays to God from the belly of the whale.

Jonah heard the voice of the Lord say to him, "Go at once to Nineveh and cry out against it, for their wickedness has come up before me."

Jonah was afraid to go to Nineveh. He tried to avoid God's plan for him. He found a ship going in the opposite direction of Nineveh and paid the sailors to take him with them.

As the ship sailed away, however, God sent a great wind and a mighty storm upon the sea. The sailors were very afraid. They cried out prayers for help. Jonah went inside the ship and tried to go to sleep.

The sailors suspected that the storm was Jonah's fault and confronted him about it. Jonah told them who he was and that he was fleeing from the Lord.

"What shall we do? How can we stop this storm now?" they said to the prophet.

Jonah looked out over the side of the boat. "Pick me up and throw me into the sea," he said. "Then the storm will quiet down. This is all my fault."

The men tried to row to safety, but there was no use. The storm was too strong. They prayed to the Lord for forgiveness and did as Jonah said. They picked him up and threw him into the water.

Suddenly the storm stopped and the waters were calm again. Jonah, however, was not safe. God sent a whale up out of the sea to swallow him.

Jonah remained alive in the belly of the whale for three days and three nights. He realized his mistake, and he was grateful to be alive. Instead of getting angry with God, he thought about all that he could be thankful for.

"I called the Lord out of my distress, and he answered me," he said. "The waters closed in over me, and my life is floating away. But I remembered the Lord, and my prayer came to him. Those who worship anything other than God forsake their loyalty."

Then he prayed, "But I with the voice of thanksgiving will worship you; what I have vowed I will pay. Deliverance belongs to the Lord!"

The Lord heard this prayer of thanksgiving. He spoke to the whale, and it spit Jonah out onto the dry land.

The Lord told Jonah again to go forth to Nineveh. This time the prophet listened. He got up and set out for the great city to preach God's message of repentance for forty days.

REFLECTION QUESTIONS

What did Jonah say to God in prayer to show he was ready to be released from the belly of the whale?

Is there anything God wants you to do right now that you are trying to avoid? What is it, and why are you afraid?

What are some things you can be thankful for even when you are sad or afraid?

THE LEPER WHO THANKED JESUS

Luke 17:11-19

It is important to give thanks and praise to God when he answers our prayers, but unfortunately, not everyone does it.

As you read this story, pay attention to what the Samaritan leper does when he realizes that Jesus has healed him.

Jesus healed many people during his travels. On the way to Jerusalem one day, he entered a village with ten lepers. They came up to him and pleaded for him to heal them.

"Jesus, Master, have mercy on us!" they said.

Jesus looked at them and said, "Go and show your-selves to the priests."

They all did as he told them and left to find a priest. As they walked away, they suddenly realized that they were healed.

One of the lepers—a Samaritan—stopped and praised God when he realized he was healed. He turned back in joy to go and find Jesus. He loudly praised God as he skipped through the village looking for him.

When he finally found Jesus, he knelt down at his feet and thanked him vigorously.

Jesus looked around. This man was the only one that returned. "Were not ten made clean? Where are the other nine? Was none of them found to return and give praise to God except this Samaritan?"

No one answered.

Jesus looked down upon the healed Samaritan at his feet. "Get up and go on your way; your faith has made you well."

REFLECTION QUESTIONS

Why did the Samaritan leper turn back to find Jesus?

What are some of the biggest reasons for you to give praise and thanks to God?

How will you remember to give God thanks and praise when he answers your prayers?

PRAYERS OF PRAISE

When you do a good job at something, you sometimes receive praise. A teacher, parent, friend, or classmate offers encouragement to say, "Good job," or, "You are good at that."

God is good. God is great. We should tell him so, just as we would praise another person for doing a good job.

God doesn't need our praise, but praising God is a gift to us and the people who hear us praise him. The following stories offer examples of people who praise God and the impact it has on those who hear those prayers.

MARY'S PRAYER OF PRAISE TO GOD

Luke 1:26–56

Mary was the Mother of God. As she says in her own prayer, she became more blessed than any other woman throughout history. She provides for us a model response to God's great blessings upon us.

As you read this story, pay attention to the way the Virgin Mary responds to God's blessing.

The angel Gabriel appeared to the young woman Mary, saying, "Hail, favored one! The Lord is with you."

Mary was confused by the angel's words and wondered what he meant by this.

The angel said to her, "Do not be afraid, Mary, for you have found favor with God. Behold, you will conceive in your womb and bear a son, and you will name him Jesus. He will be great and will be called the Son of the Most High. He will be a king, and his kingdom will have no end."

Mary said to the angel, "How can this be, since I am still unmarried and a virgin?"

The angel replied, "The Holy Spirit will come upon you, and the power of the Most High will overshadow you. The child to be born will be holy. He will be called Son of God."

Then Mary said, "Behold, I am the handmaid of the Lord. May it be done to me according to your word."

Then the angel departed from her.

Before he left, the angel told Mary that her cousin Elizabeth, who everyone thought was unable to bear children, was six months pregnant. Mary set out quickly to visit her cousin.

When Mary arrived at the house, she greeted her cousin from the door. When Elizabeth heard Mary, the unborn child leaped in her womb. Elizabeth was filled with the Holy Spirit and said, "Blessed are you among women, and blessed is the fruit of your womb. Why has this happened to me, that the mother of my Lord comes to me? Blessed is she who believed that there would be fulfillment of what was spoken to her by the Lord!"

Mary was moved by her cousin's words. She offered up her own prayer of praise, saying, "My soul magnifies the Lord, and my spirit rejoices in God my Savior, for he has looked with favor on the lowliness of his servant. Surely, from now on, all generations will call me blessed; for the Mighty One has done great things for me, and holy is his name."

REFLECTION QUESTIONS

What did Mary say in her prayer of praise to God?

What great things has God done for you, and what can you say in praise of his gifts to you?

How can you become a lowly servant of God in the way you live your life today?

A HEALED BEGGAR PRAISES THE LORD

Acts 3:1–10

When God gives us a great gift, not only can we give him thanks, we can also praise him for his wonderful deeds. After Jesus ascended up to heaven, Peter, John, and the other apostles worked many miracles that inspired many people to join them and grow the Church. These early Christians were united in their praise to God.

As you read this story, pay attention to what the crippled beggar does after Peter and John heal him in the name of the Lord.

The apostles Peter and John were on their way up to the temple to pray when they saw a group of people nearby carrying a man who could not walk. These people laid this man at the gate of the temple every day so that he could beg for money from those who went in to pray there.

As Peter and John arrived at the entrance to the temple, the crippled man begged them for money.

Peter said to the man, "Look at us."

The man fixed his attention on them, expecting them to give him some money.

But Peter said, "I have no silver or gold, but I will give you what I have. In the name of Jesus Christ, stand up and walk!"

Peter took the man by the hand and raised him up. Immediately, his feet and ankles were made strong. Not only could the man stand, he jumped up with joy!

He entered into the temple with Peter and John, leaping and praising God with great joy.

Many people heard the man praising God loudly. They looked and recognized him as the beggar from the gate to the temple. They had seen him there many times.

The people heard his praise and were filled with wonder and amazement at what God had done for him at the hands of the apostles.

REFLECTION QUESTIONS

What did the man do after God healed him through the apostles?

Who have you seen offer prayers of praise to God?

How can you praise God for the great things he has done for you?

THE PEOPLE PRAISE GOD IN HEAVEN

Revelation 5

God gave John a vision of the heavens that he recorded in the book of Revelation. In this vision, he saw Jesus in the form of a lamb. Lambs were sacrificed by God's people in the Old Testament for forgiveness of sins. The blood of the lamb was also used during the Passover.

As you read this story, pay attention to the words of the song that the angels and saints sing to the Lamb of God.

John saw the Lord sitting on a throne, holding a scroll with seven seals, and an angel proclaiming in a loud voice, "Who is worthy to open the scroll and break its seals?"

John looked around. There was no one there in heaven or on Earth who was worthy to open the scroll or look into it. This made John weep.

Then he saw a lamb standing before the scroll. The lamb went and took the scroll from the right hand of the one on the throne.

All the creatures and elders in heaven bowed down before the lamb. They held harps and bowls full of incense to offer their prayers to God.

They sang a new song, which began, "You are worthy to take the scroll and to open its seals."

Then John heard the voices of thousands of angels surrounding the throne joining in a song:

"Worthy is the Lamb that was slain to receive power and wealth and wisdom and might and honor and glory and blessing!"

Then the song continued, and every creature in heaven and earth joined in singing:

"To the one seated on the throne of the Lamb be blessing and honor and glory and might for ever and ever!"

Then they ended their song and said, "Amen!"

REFLECTION QUESTIONS

What did the angels and saints sing about the Lamb of God?

How can we give Jesus (the Lamb of God) honor and glory in our lives?

What are the good things that God has done in the world that give you a reason to praise him?

PRAYERS OF BLESSING

When we are blessed, God is with us. A prayer to bless is a prayer to recognize and ask for God's presence here on Earth.

The following stories offer examples of people who asked for God's blessing upon others. These blessings gave them the gifts they needed to overcome their greatest challenges.

MELCHIZEDEK BLESSES ABRAHAM

Genesis 14:17–20

The priests in the Old Testament offered prayers of blessing to the Lord. A blessing invokes God's presence here on Earth. The priest King Melchizedek appears briefly in the book of Genesis, but he was remembered by Jews and Christians for centuries with great honor.

As you read this story, pay attention to Abraham's response to the blessing of Melchizedek.

Abram, who God later renamed Abraham, went into battle to rescue his nephew Lot. He won the battle, saved his nephew, and then returned home.

Melchizedek was the king and high priest of Salem, which is now the city of Jerusalem. He came to bless Abram after the battle. He brought with him bread and wine. He blessed Abram with these words:

"Blessed be Abram by God Most High, maker of heaven and earth; and blessed be God Most High, who has delivered your enemies into your hand."

Abram was very grateful for the blessing. He was so grateful that he gave the high priest one tenth of all the riches he won during the battle.

REFLECTION QUESTIONS

Abram gave the high priest 10 percent of everything he won in the battle. How can you give some of your money or time to the Church in return for the blessings laid upon you?

Who are the people in your life who you would like to bless?

Why do you think we bless our food before we eat it?

MOSES BLESSES JOSHUA

Numbers 27:12-23; Deuteronomy 31:1-8

A blessing is more than a prayer with kind words. A blessing gives us true courage and wisdom from God. When we are blessed by God, we have no need to fear, because God is with us.

As you read this story, pay attention to what Joshua receives from God through Moses's prayer of blessing over him as the new leader of the people of Israel.

Moses led the people of Israel out of slavery in Egypt and through the wilderness, but he knew he would not lead them into the Promised Land. He had disobeyed and disappointed God. Because of this, the Lord told him he would not go any farther with his people.

So Moses prayed to God, saying, "Let the Lord appoint someone over the congregation who shall go out before them and come in before them, who shall lead them out and bring them in, so that the congregation of the Lord may not be like a sheep without a shepherd."

The Lord said in reply, "Take Joshua son of Nun, a man in whom is the spirit, and lay your hands upon him. Have him stand before the priest and all the congregation to commission him in their sight. You shall give him some of your authority."

Moses did as the Lord commanded. He took Joshua and had him stand before Eleazar the priest and all of the people of Israel. He laid his hands on him and blessed him.

Years later, as Moses was nearing death, he gathered the people of Israel together. He announced to them, "I am now very old. I am no longer able to get about easily. I have led you out of the land of Egypt, but I will not lead you into the Promised Land. The Lord has told me that I will not cross over the Jordan River."

The people gasped in shock. They had looked to Moses as their leader for so many years. They wondered how they could go on without him.

Moses continued, "The Lord your God himself will cross over before you. He will protect you from your enemies. Joshua also will cross over before you, as the Lord has promised. Under his leadership, you will win the battles against your enemies. Be strong and bold; have no fear or dread of them, because it is the Lord your God who goes with you. He will not fail you or forsake you."

Then Moses called Joshua forward from the crowd. In front of all the people of Israel, Moses prayed a blessing over Joshua, saying, "Be strong and bold, for you are the one who will go with this people into the land that the Lord has promised to them. It is the Lord who goes before you. He will be with you. He will not fail or forsake you. Do not fear or be dismayed."

Not long after extending this blessing upon Joshua, Moses died. Joshua took up the role of leader of God's people. He was filled with the spirit of wisdom because Moses had laid his hands on him.

REFLECTION QUESTIONS

What gifts did Joshua receive from God through Moses's prayer of blessing over him?

Who could you go to in order to ask for God's blessing in your life right now (parents, pastors, priests, teachers, or other family members)?

What challenges lie before you, and how could God's blessing help you get through those challenges?

SAMUEL ANOINTS DAVID AS KING

1 Samuel 16:1–13

God does not look on us as we see each other. We might think that God blesses those who are strong, but the Lord blesses those whom he will strengthen and who will accept his help.

As you read this story, pay attention to the reasons that the Lord withheld his blessing from the older sons of Jesse.

God was disappointed in Saul, the king of Israel. He told the prophet Samuel to anoint another person as king.

The Lord said to the prophet, "Fill your horn with oil. Go to Bethlehem, where you will find a man named Jesse. I have provided for myself a king from among his sons."

So Samuel traveled to Bethlehem and invited Jesse and his sons to a blessing ceremony. The father and his boys joined Samuel as he requested.

First, Jesse brought forth his oldest son, Eliab.

Samuel saw the young man and thought to himself, "Surely this is the one the Lord wants me to anoint as king."

But the Lord said to Samuel, "Do not look on his appearance or on his height, because I have rejected him; for the Lord does not see as humans see. Humans look on the outward appearance, but the Lord looks on the heart."

Jesse called another son up to bring before Samuel, but the Lord said to him, "Neither has the Lord chosen this one."

Jesse brought seven of his sons before Samuel, but the Lord said that none of them were his chosen one.

Finally, Samuel said to Jesse, "Are all your sons here?"

Jesse said, "No, there is one more, my youngest son, David. He is out in the fields, keeping the sheep."

"Send for him and bring him to me," the prophet instructed.

Jesse sent for David, who arrived soon afterward. He had rosy cheeks and beautiful eyes. He was very handsome.

Suddenly, the Lord said to Samuel, "Rise, and anoint him; for this is the one."

The prophet Samuel took the horn of oil and anointed the youngest son in the presence of all of his older brothers. The spirit of the Lord came mightily upon David from that day forward.

REFLECTION QUESTIONS

Why did the Lord wish to bless and anoint David and not his older brothers?

Why do you think it is so difficult to look on the heart of other people rather than their outward appearance?

In what ways can you become humble so that God can bless you?

ABOUT BIBLE BREAKS

The Bible Breaks stories for kids help families and faith formation groups set aside a few minutes during the day to read and reflect on the Word of God. Each short and simple story is written to help teach children the most important lessons of the Christian life from sacred Scripture.

Learn more at jareddees.com/biblebreaks

ALSO BY JARED DEES

Jared Dees is the author of numerous books, including a short story collection titled *Beatitales: 80 Fables about the Beatitudes for Children*.

Download a collection of these stories at jareddees.com/beatitales.

BOOKS BY JARED DEES

31 Days to Becoming a Better Religious Educator

To Heal, Proclaim, and Teach

Praying the Angelus

Christ in the Classroom

Beatitales

Tales of the Ten Commandments

Do Not Be Afraid

Take and Eat

ABOUT THE AUTHOR

Jared Dees is the creator of *TheReligionTeacher.com*, a popular website that provides practical resources and teaching strategies to religious educators. A respected graduate of the Alliance for Catholic Education (ACE) program at the University of Notre Dame, Dees holds master's degrees in education and theology, both from Notre Dame. He frequently gives keynotes and leads workshops at conferences, church events, and school in-services throughout the year on a variety of topics. He lives near South Bend, Indiana, with his wife and children.

Learn more about Jared's books, speaking events, and other projects at jareddees.com.

www.ingramcontent.com/pod-product-compliance
Lightning Source LLC
Chambersburg PA
CBHW070831050426
42452CB00011B/2241